BIBS
Daily Devotional

(Name) HAILEY NOEL KNOUF

Book Contents

START HERE 5
Commitment 6

HOW TO USE THIS BOOK 7
Observation 12
Interpretation 13
Application 16

Appendix 1 – Sources 74
Appendix 2 – Genres 75
Appendix 3 – Examples 76
Why Read the Bible? 78
BIBS Wall 85

Week 1 (Philemon)	20
Week 2 (Psalms)	25
Week 3	30
Week 4 (Ephesians)	36
Week 5	41
Week 6	46
Week 7 (Nehemiah)	52
Week 8	58
Week 9	63
Week 10	68

The BIBS Devotional Book is a daily Bible reading and study plan. It is designed to guide the reader daily through an in-depth study of a short passage and a weekly overview of the surrounding chapters.

Note from the author: There are two main reasons I rarely recommend devotional books for teens. First, they cater to the false idea that teens need things "dumbed down" for them to understand. Wrong! Teens are motivated to excel at whatever they are challenged to do. BIBS challenges them to know their Bibles. If they are up to the task, they will excel.

Second, in most devotionals, the reader reads too little of the Bible and thinks too little for himself. God's Word IS saying something in every text, but discovering it for myself and applying it to myself is what I need most.

Following the BIBS format offers both the depths of Scripture AND the flow of thought of the context of Scripture. It is a guide to help you hear from God and a tool to help you understand and apply His desires for your life.

PREFACE TO THIS EDITION

I was listening to a podcast recently about a fitness business that "levels you up" like a video game for each tier you reach. I thought that was pretty cool. I'm not a video gamer, but I'm a board gamer, and leveling up my character sounded awesome!

I hired my sister-in-law **Anna Rench** to sketch me some characters and . . . voilà . . . we have character upgrades in the *BIBS Devotional*. As you progress, your character "levels up" in power.

This edition of the *BIBS Devotional* is simpler, easier to understand, and launches you right into a "quick win." In one week, you will have gone in-depth on a book of the Bible you might never have considered before.

This "Starter Edition" is perfect for anyone looking to build the habit of Bible study into their lives. The simple and fun format will keep you engaged in God's Word like you have never been before.

Ready to launch into it? Let's go!

Copyright © 2018 by:
Calvary Baptist Publications | Temecula, CA.

All Scripture quotations are taken from the King James Version.

All rights reserved. No part of this publication may be reproduced, distributed, or transmitted in any form or by any means, including photocopying, recording, or other electronic or mechanical methods, without the prior written permission of the publisher, except in the case of brief quotations embodied in critical reviews and certain other noncommercial uses permitted by copyright law. For permission requests, write to the publisher, addressed "Attention: Permissions Coordinator," at the address below.

Calvary Baptist Publications
31087 Nicolas Rd. Temecula, CA 92591
(951) 676–8700 | calvarybaptist.pub

The Bible is all that will matter...

Before getting into the BIBS Devotional, you have to first know that the Bible is the only thing that will matter in 246 years. It's the only thing that can protect you from the nasty messes in life. Seems crazy NOT to read it!

Personal discipline

Are you disciplined enough to study the Bible without someone forcing you to do it? If so, the next few weeks will be amazing.

People commit to band, martial arts, sports practice or even school... but will you commit to spiritual growth? This Bible study will outlast everything else in your life, so take it seriously. At LEAST commit to <u>one month</u>. It could take as little as 15 minutes per day.

Commit now?

Will you commit right now?

A Daily and Weekly Devotional

1. Commit to 1 month

Lord, with your help, I commit to one month of Bible study.

_____

(Signature)

When and where?

If you made that commitment, write the time and location you'll do your devotions every day:

_____

(Time)   (Location)

2. Full commitment of my mind

Are you willing to go past one month and complete this book? If you will <u>honestly work and think</u> and not just "get by," then sign your name below.

Notice, you're **not** committing to:

- Filling out every line
- Getting every answer right
- Daily work (because then if you miss one day you feel like you've failed God!)

You **are** committing to be honest before God and sincerely asking Him to make this Bible study something that will help you.

God, before You and only with Your help, I commit to <u>honestly work</u> to make this something valuable to my spiritual life.

_____

(Signature)   (Date)

That's it! This is between you and God now!

Always remember, "...a just man falleth seven times, and riseth up again." (Proverbs 24:16) You'll probably miss a day or two here and there, but DON'T let that discourage you. If this is new to you, **it may take about three weeks to get into the habit**.

Stick it out. By the fourth week it will be much easier. Soon, if it's *real*, you won't be able to put your Bible *down*. That's a much better problem than never picking it up!

How to use this book

 **Weekly**

Each week is designed to give you the broad overview of the context, and to help you get into the author's flow of thought. It involves all three steps of the BIBS format (Observation, Interpretation, Application).

Each week will keep you both in large and small portions of Scripture. This gives you the in-depth study of a particular text as well as the "birds-eye view" through several chapters at a time (discussed below).

 **Daily**

Daily reading and writing are what the BIBS format is all about. Each day will be a different assignment than the day before, although each day will also repeat information from the week.

Some days will be mostly reading, some will be writing, and some will be thinking. Don't try to do every step in one day. The BIBS format is spread over a week for a reason. You'll have plenty of time to complete each part. (But if you do work ahead... that's okay too!)

A Daily and Weekly Devotional 7

As a Journal

Journals force you to articulate your thoughts into coherent sentences. We can all have the "I want to do more for God" moments, but what does that mean?

Sometimes your mind gets jumbled up in a tangle of thoughts about God, but until you unravel them through writing *words*, even you might not know exactly what you are thinking.

Blank lines flank both sides of the BIBS Devotional, and you can use them in a variety of ways:

- Add "overflow" info from the BIBS studies
- Write a daily thought about God
- Write a prayer out each day
- Create a "Spiritual To-Do List" based on the Application Days
- Write two things you are thankful for each day
- Write about your day
- Track your prayer requests
- Write one funny thing you heard that day
- Take sermon notes

The possibilities are nearly endless. You are an author, even if you don't have a book yet. This journal can be your first.

As a Coloring Book?

Sure! For each day you complete, shade in a brick on the BIBS Wall. Get creative! Share your masterpiece with #BIBSwall and watch your fortress grow. Bonus points for 3D shading.

See the back of the book for your #BIBSwall.

WHAT'S "BIBS?"

BIBS: Big Idea Bible Study

Why call it the Big Idea Bible Study? Think of the Big Idea this way:

A thank-you card has a specific intent: thanking someone for something.

A letter of recommendation has a specific intent: recommending someone or something.

A love letter has a specific and single intent: wishing someone a happy birthday. (Wait... what?! No.)

When you sit to write any kind of note or draft some sort of business letter, there is almost always a specific and single reason. Letters and notes usually say only one thing: "Thank you," "I recommend...," or "I love you." for example.

The body of the letter has lots of *things* say, but all those *things* as a whole combine to say only one thing.

Deep and wide

Bible study is both deep and wide. Sometimes people get lost in the "depths" of Scripture and at other times they breeze so quickly through the chapters that they miss the gold nuggets along the way.

To me, the best times in my life are when I am deep in God's Word.

However, I cannot truly get deeper into a biblical text until I've read several chapters before and after it and got into the biblical author's flow of thought.

Bible study needs both—both the depths of the text AND the full context (or flow) of the biblical author's thoughts.

So?

The Big Idea Bible Study is designed to be both an **in-depth** look at certain portions of Scripture as well as a **birds-eye view** of the biblical text. As you study, you will discover:

- What the author's original intent was
- What the timeless truth is
- What it means for us today

God's ideas blossom from the text into rich truths. Our job is to work on finding them (Observation & Interpretation) and then obeying them (through Application).

ROCKS
It is easier to catch a rock than a handful of sand. The Bible is not full of a bunch of unrelated thoughts (sand). It is full of ideas... rocks!

Say! What's the BIG IDEA?

3 STEPS
TO VIEW EVERY TEXT

Taken from Howard Hendricks' *Living By the Book*, each Bible text needs to be viewed three ways: OBSERVATION, INTERPRETATION, and APPLICATION. Bookmark or dog-ear these pages to refer back to them for the first few weeks. They'll help you when you're stuck.

OBSERVATION
THE BIRDS-EYE VIEW

INTERPRETATION
WHAT IS GOD SAYING?

APPLICATION
WHAT IS GOD SAYING TO ME?

A Daily and Weekly Devotional

OBSERVATION

The birds-eye view

The first view, OBSERVATION, is the broad overview of what's going on in the text. It's as if you're flying way up in the sky and surveying the whole land (although I doubt this fat little bird can fly!). Ask broad questions:

- Why was the book written in the first place?
- What happened in this story before this text?
- To whom is it written?
- What's the problem with mankind that God is trying to fix with this text? (It HAS to address some need... what is it?)
- What *type* of writing is it?
    - Narrative – A broad, often long story with a lesson or moral.
    - Law – God's commandments for His people Israel.
    - Prophets – Warnings from God to His people Israel.
    - Psalms – Songs and prayers to or about God.
    - Wisdom – Proverbs and poetry.
    - Gospels – The story of Christ from different perspectives.
    - Acts – A history of the church in transition.
    - Parable – A story with a single point.
    - Epistle – A letter to a church or individual.
    - Prophecy – Foretelling of judgments and hope.
    - For more information on genres, see **Appendix 2.**

INTERPRETATION

What is God saying?

The second view, INTERPRETATION, answers the basic question, "What is God saying?" What was God fixing or teaching or encouraging or commanding *the first readers* to do?

God does not change. If we know what He *said,* we can know what God is *saying.* That is INTERPRETATION, and here are a few steps to help you find that Big Idea:

1. Read

Your best tool will be reading. Read through the text (the small "chunk" of Scripture) and try to get a broad idea of what it's saying.

2. Reread

Now, go back and read those few verses again. Think harder this time. Try to get an overall idea of what's going on.

3. Flag Words

Use a Bible Dictionary, a *Strong's Concordance*, an online Bible or an app that defines confusing words for you. As you read, look up words to help you understand what the Bible is saying.

"What am I talking about?"

Sit down next to Paul or Peter or Daniel or David. Imagine them asking, "What am I talking about?"

What's their text about? Sin? Cheating? Love? Singing? God? Satan? Don't get lost in the details yet... think BIG idea.

If the BIG IDEA is like a tree, then start with the trunk:

4. Word

What one word comes to mind as an overall thought for this text (see Appendix 3 for examples)?

5. Phrase

Now, suppose that one word is *Praise*. **Narrow that down** a little. Is this text saying everything about praise? No. Whose praise? Who is praising? What about praise? What kind of praise?

Suppose our phrase is *Praise of God*. That's narrower, but it's still not enough. Go further...

6. Sentence

Expand that phrase into a sentence. What about praising God?

Don't come up with the sentence on your own. Base it on the text.

The sentence: "We should praise the Lord" is a complete thought. It is definite. It is concise. It is a rock.

Tools of the trade

Some good tools for observation and interpretation are a simple Bible reference tool for your computer, a Bible dictionary and/or a study Bible. Free Bible software can be downloaded at www.e-sword.net. Or, several online sources will have Strongs reference numbers. Good dictionaries such as Webster's 1828 can be referenced online, and a good study Bible will give you an overview of the book, cross references, maps, and further explanations as you read.

Warning: use man's wisdom sparingly! Your goal is to hear from God, so don't rely on these Bible study tools to "get the right answer." You're not after the "right answer." You must hear from God, so spend most of your time in His Word!

"WHAT AM I SAYING ABOUT WHAT I'M TALKING ABOUT?"

Fill in the branches of your tree (Big Idea). These "branches" are the details that say stuff about what you found in earlier steps.

7. Question word

If you could turn your sentence into a question, what **question word** would you use? Is this a **who, what, where, when, why** or **how** text?

Question

Rearrange your sentence into a question. Example:

"**Why** should we praise the Lord?"

8. Answer(s)

Once you have the question, **answer it from the text.** The answers you find will fill out your tree with all its beauty.

"Why should we praise the Lord?" Psalm 117 gives two "branches":

- Because his merciful kindness is great toward us.
- Because the truth of the Lord endureth forever.

Application

What is God saying <u>to me</u>?

There's only one *interpretation* to each passage—only one right meaning. BUT... when it comes to APPLICATION (what God is saying <u>to me</u>) there are tons of ways this could go!

Overall, what did you learn?

God speaks in SO many different ways through His Word, and maybe He spoke to you from one little phrase, the whole "Big Idea," or even just in one word you studied. How did He speak to you through this text? How does it apply to you? What did you learn? How has it helped or encouraged or challenged you?

Application days

It's easy to learn stuff about God. It's easy to know you're supposed to watch your mouth, be in church, obey your parents, etc. The Bible is easy to know, but HARD to do.

Every "Application Day" will need to be a serious time between you and God. First, pray and ask Him to reveal hidden sin. Next, ask Him to help you overcome it. Finally, ask Him if there's even anything small in your life that could be changed. He will reveal "big" and "small" sins in your life, and it is your job to change them through His power.

"Application Days" come around a couple times per week in the BIBS format and should be a clear-minded, open-hearted soul searching time before God.

Self deception

But be ye doers of the word and not hearers only, **deceiving your own selves.** *James 1:22*

Are you deceived right now? You don't know. According to James 1:22, the more you hear the Word and don't do anything about it, the more self-deceived you become. Scary!

DO something!

Determine to not only know stuff about the Bible but to actually do stuff with your knowledge. If the "Big Idea" you find is something like, "We should praise the Lord because His mercy is great toward us and His truth endures forever," you can respond a couple different ways:

"That's nice. David praised God. What a swell guy. Time for school!"

Or…

"Wow, God is merciful to ME. I know me… God, thank you. I want to live for you."

And, "God, thank you for your truth that I can read today. Thank you for sharing your mind with me so I never have to wonder. Religions try to please their gods with sacrifices, always wondering if it's enough. Thank you for the Truth of your Word."

And, "God, your kindness and truth are GREAT toward me. Thank you for the abundant life you provide me even now. I'm humbled by your great goodness."

I'll praise you more through prayer and singing this week!

Make a plan

Once you've decided to do something, write out your plan. **Be specific.**

Example:

So that I am not deceived, I plan to:

-Sing so loud at church on Sunday that people think I've lost it.

-Not care what people think

-Buy a hymnal and slowly read one hymn per day

-Add "Thank God for his mercy and truth" to my daily prayers

Conclude in prayer

God's been speaking and you've been responding by promising to act on His Word. Now conclude in prayer and ask God's help and strength as you do what you committed to do. (Dan. 1:8)

BIBS SUMMARY

Follow these steps and you should have a pretty good idea of what God is saying to you:

1. Read
2. Reread
3. Flag Words

TRUNK
4. Boil Down to a Word
5. Expand to a Phrase
6. Summarize in a Sentence

BRANCHES
7. Rephrase into a Question
8. Answer the Question
9. Combine into a Sentence
10. Apply the Truth

Daily Checklist

The following list is the basic idea for how each day might look:

 DAY 1 Reading Day (Observation)
1. Pray
2. Study Bible – read intro paragraph
3. Read whole book (or large portion)
4. Note text 1 & 2

 DAY 2 Rereading Day
1. Read 2 chapters
2. Reread text 1
3. One word
4. Phrase

 DAY 3 Thinking Day (Interpretation)
1. Read 2 chapters
2. Reread text 1
3. Review yesterday's phrase
4. Expand to a sentence (tree trunk)
5. Turn it into a question (what question word?)
6. Answer the question (branches)

 DAY 4 Application Day (Application)
1. Read full chapter
2. Combine "Trunk" and "Branches"
3. What is God saying? (BIG IDEA – full tree)
4. What is God saying TO ME? Application.
5. Write plan

 DAY 5 Rereading Day
1. Read 2 chapters
2. Reread text 2
3. One word
4. Phrase

 DAY 6 Thinking Day (Interpretation)
1. Read 2 chapters
2. Reread text 2
3. Review yesterday's phrase
4. Expand to a sentence (tree trunk)
5. Turn it into a question (what question word?)
6. Answer the question (branches)

 DAY 7 Application Day (Application)
1. Read full chapter
2. Combine "Trunk" and "Branches"
3. What is God saying? (BIG IDEA – full tree)
4. What is God saying TO ME? Application.
5. Write plan
6. Discuss texts 1 & 2 in church

Ready to get going? *God, please help us as we learn your will through your Word.*

Journal *Daily add things you are thankful for, thoughts about God, and anything else.*

PHILEMON
WEEK 1

For background material, search a study Bible, a Bible Encyclopedia, a Bible commentary or a Bible Handbook. These types of books will give you the overview of the book and a few topics to look for as you read.

Philemon was a rich Christian whose slave, Onesimus, ran away and stole household goods. Onesimus got saved, and Paul sent him back to Philemon, promising to pay for anything that Onesimus stole and trusting that Philemon would love his new brother in Christ (Onesimus) enough to forgive him.

The book of Philemon is the letter that Onesimus carried to his old master.

DAY 1
Reading Day (Observation)

1. Pray. Open in prayer. Ask God's forgiveness for known sin and ask for His help in today's study.

2. Background. If you have a study tool (online source, study Bible, computer software, commentary...), read some background on the book. Write some things you learned here (see p. 12 andAppendix 3 for some ideas.):

_____

3. Read Philemon. Read the whole book (one chapter) to get the overall concept.

4. Note the text divisions. See what's coming up this week. Write the two texts you'll be studying below (this time it's done for you):

PHILEMON 1:1-7; PHILEMON 1:8-25

5. VICTORY! Go build your #BIBSwall. You completed a day. AWESOME! Go to the back of the book and fill in one (1) brick. You'll start as the Digger, but don't worry . . . keep at it and soon you'll get an upgrade.

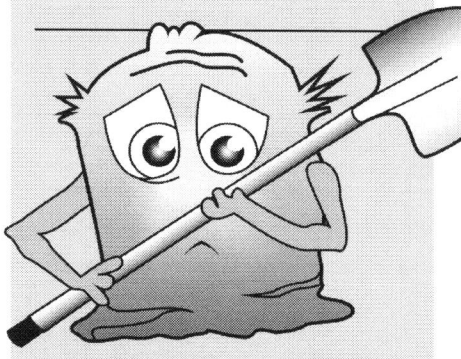

CONGRATS! You're a Digger.
(color **1 brick** per day)

As a digger, you dig. That's all. Dig dirt. Throw it in a pile. Load a wheelbarrow. Move it. Dump it. Dig it again.

That's why you look sad. You need an upgrade. Keep working, and maybe you'll get a better job.

20   B.I.B.S. - Big Idea Bible Study

DAY 2
Rereading Day

1. Pray.

2. Read. Read Philemon.

3. Reread text. Read 1:1–7.

4. Word. What word generally describes this text (1:1–7)?

_____

5. Phrase. Now what about that word? Expand it to a phrase:

_____

6. Second Day . . . DONE! You're on a roll. Keep it up. Now go build your #BIBSwall. Color one more brick in.

DAY 3
Thinking Day (Interpretation)

1. Pray.

2. Read. Read Philemon.

3. Reread text. Read 1:1–7.

4. Sentence. Expand yesterday's phrase to a sentence:

_____

5. Question. If that sentence could be turned into a question, what word could be used (who, what, where, when, why, how)? Rewrite the sentence in the form of a question:

_____

6. Answer(s). Write the answers to your question below. These answers are all the ideas taken from the text.

_____

7. It's #BIBSwall time. Go color in a brick. That's 3 down!

Journal *Continued*

_____

A Daily and Weekly Devotional   21

Journal *Daily add things you are thankful for, thoughts about God, and anything else.*

DAY 4
Application Day

1. Pray.

2. Read. Read Philemon.

3. Combine. Try to combine the "Trunk" (sentence/question) and the "Branches" (answers) into a complete thought here:

_____
_____

4. Apply. The BIG IDEA you just wrote is what God said. And that's what He's still saying. So now… what is He saying <u>to you</u>?

First, write some general things you learned:

_____
_____
_____
_____
_____

Next, whether you learned it from one word, the big idea, or even some random, obscure thought you had, write any other application you can think of:

_____
_____
_____
_____
_____

5. Plan. Write your plan to DO something different in your life because of what you have learned.

So that I am not deceived, I plan to:

_____
_____
_____
_____
_____

6. Color time. Good digging, so far! Go shade in another brick.

DAY 5
Rereading Day

1. Pray.

2. Read. Read Philemon.

3. Reread text. Read 1:8–25.

4. Word. What word generally describes this text?

_____

5. Phrase. Now what about that word? Expand it to a phrase:

_____
_____

6. Five days down. Finish the week strong. Two days left. Go color your brick! *Fun fact: 9+6=3 (How? Find out on Day 7)*

DAY 6
Thinking Day (Interpretation)

1. Pray.

2. Read. Read Philemon.

3. Reread text. Read 1:8–25 (especially 9, 15, 18, 21).

4. Sentence. Now expand yesterday's phrase to a sentence:

_____
_____

5. Question. If that sentence could be turned into a question, circle the word that could be used (who, what, where, when, why, how).

Now rewrite the sentence in the form of a question:

_____
_____

6. Answer(s). Write the many answers to your question below. These answers are all the ideas taken from the text.

_____
_____
_____

7. Almost a WEEK done. You're amazing. Go color a brick!

Journal *Continued*

A Daily and Weekly Devotional 23

Journal *Daily add things you are thankful for, thoughts about God, and anything else.*

DAY 7
Application Day

1. Pray.

2. Read. Read Philemon.

3. Combine. Try to combine the "Trunk" and the "Branches" into a complete thought here (like Day 4):

_____
_____

4. Apply. The BIG IDEA you just wrote is what God said. And that's what He's still saying. So now... what is He saying to you?

First, write some general things you learned.

_____
_____
_____
_____
_____

Next, whether you learned it from one word, the big idea, or even some random, obscure thought you had, write any other application you can think of:

_____
_____
_____
_____

5. Plan. Write your plan to DO something different in your life because of what you have learned.

So that I am not deceived, I plan to:

_____
_____
_____

6. You are a Bible super-human! You finished the week like a champ! Great work. Not too many people can stick to a new habit, but you did! Go build your #BIBSwall.

7. JOURNAL REVIEW. Read over your journal. It was a great week! (see page 8 for new journaling ideas for next week)

Fun fact ANSWER (from Day 5): 9+6=3?
Think of the face of a clock: 9 (o' clock) + 6 (hours) = 3 (o' clock)

24   B.I.B.S. - Big Idea Bible Study

Psalms
WEEK 2

Psalms are songs about our relationship with God. They are emotional and filled with expressive language.

Psalms is broken into five books. Book One includes David's time of running from Saul and is sometimes forlorn. Book Two includes songs from David's kingdom, while Book Three and Book Four cover Israel's crisis time. Book Five covers Israel's release from exile, and is reflective and exciting.

Psalms are personal and passionate. Find yourself in the Psalms and learn to talk with God friend to friend. Be real with Him. You'll be surprised how real David and the other Psalmists are in the texts you will read coming up...

DAY 1
Reading Day (Observation)

1. Pray. Open in prayer. Ask God's forgiveness for known sin and ask for His help in today's study.

2. Background. If you have a study tool (online source, study Bible, computer software, commentary...), read some background on the book. Write some things you learned here (see p. 12 and Appendix 3 for some ideas.):

___

3. Read a bunch. Read several Psalms to get a bigger picture of what God is saying about creation: Psalms 8, 19, 29, 65, and 104.

4. Note the text divisions. See what's coming up this week. Write the two texts you'll be studying below:

___

5. UPGRADED! You're now in Week Two. Boom. Two stones per day. You'll have that #BIBSwall done in no time.

Fun fact: Psalms is the only book that does not call its divisions "chapters."

Journal Continued

___

YOU'VE BEEN UPGRADED!
You're now a Stone Grunt.
*(color **2 bricks** per day!)*

It's not glamorous, but working on the wall is better than digging–you're a builder now.

Er... you're cutting, shaping and hauling rocks, but hey, now you can do TWO bricks per day! And, you'll be ripped...

A Daily and Weekly Devotional   25

Journal *Daily add things you are thankful for, thoughts about God, and anything else.*

_____
_____
_____
_____
_____
_____
_____
_____
_____
_____
_____
_____
_____
_____
_____
_____
_____
_____
_____
_____
_____
_____
_____
_____
_____
_____
_____

DAY 2
Rereading Day

1. Pray.

2. Read. Read Psalms 19, 8, and 29.

3. Reread text. Read Psalm 19.

4. Word. What word generally describes this text (19:1–14)?

_____

5. Phrase. Now what about that word? Expand it to a phrase:

_____
_____

6. And . . . Cut! Easy 'nuf. Time to shade TWO bricks.

DAY 3
Thinking Day (Interpretation)

1. Pray.

2. Read. Read Psalm 19, 65, and 104.

3. Reread text. Read 19.

4. Sentence. Expand yesterday's phrase to a sentence:

_____
_____

5. Question. If that sentence could be turned into a question, what word could be used (who, what, where, when, why, how)? Rewrite the sentence in the form of a question:

_____
_____

6. Answer(s). Write the answers to your question below. These answers are all the ideas taken from the text.

_____
_____
_____

7. It's #BIBSwall time. Go color in two bricks. That's almost half a row!

26   B.I.B.S. - Big Idea Bible Study

DAY 4
Application Day

1. Pray.

2. Read. Read Psalm 19.

3. Combine. Try to combine the "Trunk" (sentence/question) and the "Branches" (answers) into a complete thought here:

_____
_____

4. Apply. The BIG IDEA you just wrote is what God said. And that's what He's still saying. So now... what is He saying <u>to you</u>?

First, write some general things you learned:

_____
_____
_____
_____

Next, whether you learned it from one word, the big idea, or even some random, obscure thought you had, write any other application you can think of:

_____
_____
_____
_____

5. Plan. Write your plan to DO something different in your life because of what you have learned.

So that I am not deceived, I plan to:

_____
_____
_____
_____

6. Colorfest. Good building, so far! Go shade in two more bricks.

Journal *Continued*

A Daily and Weekly Devotional 27

Journal *Daily add things you are thankful for, thoughts about God, and anything else.*

_____
_____
_____
_____
_____
_____
_____
_____
_____
_____
_____
_____
_____
_____
_____
_____
_____
_____
_____
_____
_____
_____
_____
_____
_____
_____
_____
_____

DAY 5
Reading Day

1. Pray.

2. Read. Read 2 Samuel 11–12 and then Psalm 51.

3. Reread text. Reread Psalm 51.

4. Word. What word generally describes this text?

_____

5. Phrase. Now what about that word? Expand it to a phrase:

_____

_____

6. Build the wall! Finish the week strong. Color two bricks.

RANDOMNOPOLOUSOPOLY: What phrases are represented? (use the first letter of each word) (wait until Day 7 for answer)

Example: **S**ound **C**ereal **P**roduces: S_____ C_____ P_____ (*poP, elkcarC, panS*, Rice Krispies)*

Flavorful, Leaking Grease! (KFC)_____

*Adapted from <u>Crowd Pleasing Puzzles</u> book by Patrick Berry and Todd McClary.

DAY 6
Thinking Day (Interpretation)

1. Pray.

2. Read. Read 2 Samuel 12:1–25 and Psalm 51.

3. Reread text. Reread Psalm 51.

4. Sentence. Now expand yesterday's phrase to a sentence:

_____

_____

5. Question. If that sentence could be turned into a question, what word could be used (who, what, where, when, why, how)? Rewrite the sentence in the form of a question:

_____

_____

6. Answer(s). Write the many answers to your question below. These answers are all the ideas taken from the text.

_____
_____
_____

7. Almost TWO WEEKS done. That's a fortnight. What a champ. Go color two bricks!

DAY 7
Application Day

1. Pray.

2. Read. Read Psalm 51.

3. Combine. Try to combine the "Trunk" and the "Branches" into a complete thought here (like Day 4):

_____
_____
_____

4. Apply. The BIG IDEA you just wrote is what God said. And that's what He's still saying. So now... what is He saying <u>to you</u>?

First, write some general things you learned.

_____
_____
_____
_____
_____

Next, whether you learned it from one word, the big idea, or even some random, obscure thought you had, write any other application you can think of:

_____
_____
_____
_____

Journal Continued

Journal *Daily add things you are thankful for, thoughts about God, and anything else.*

_____
_____
_____
_____
_____
_____
_____
_____
_____
_____
_____
_____
_____
_____
_____
_____
_____
_____
_____
_____
_____
_____
_____
_____
_____

5. Plan. Write your plan to DO something different in your life because of what you have learned.

So that I am not deceived, I plan to:

_____
_____
_____
_____
_____
_____

6. You have joined an elite club. I call you the "fortnighters." Two straight weeks of Bible study. Time to celebrate. #BIBSwall

7. JOURNAL REVIEW. Read over your journal. God's so good. (see page 8 for more journaling ideas for next week)

RANDOMNOPOLOUSOPOLY ANSWER (from Day 5): Finger Lickin' Good (KFC)

Psalms (CONTINUED)
WEEK 3

DAY 1
Reading Day (Observation)

1. Pray. Open in prayer. Ask God's forgiveness for known sin and ask for His help in today's study.

2. Background. If you have a study tool (online source, study Bible, computer software, commentary…), read some more background on the book or on the upcoming chapters. Write some things you learned here (see p. 12 and Appendix 3 for some ideas.):

_____
_____
_____
_____
_____

3. Get the context. Read several Psalms to see how they fit together. Read Psalms 138–145.

30   B.I.B.S. - Big Idea Bible Study

4. Note the text divisions. See what's coming up this week. Write the two texts you'll be studying below:

_____

5. UPGRADE TIME! Week three? You deserve a promotion! You've done a fine job as a Digger and a Stone Grunt . . . Now you get to be a Water Hauler! You're crucial to the stability of these walls. You now earn THREE bricks per day toward your wall. Congratulations. This wall needs you.

Fun fact: pick up a handful of sand and count the grains. Each speck counts as a thought God has toward you! (139:17–18)

DAY 2
Rereading Day

1. Pray.

2. Read. Read Psalms 138–140.

3. Reread text. Read Psalm 139.

4. Word. What word generally describes this text (139:1–24)?

_____

5. Phrase. Now what about that word? Expand it to a phrase:

_____
_____

6. Glug, glug, glug. . . Hey, are you drinking that water? Get back to work. *wink. Good work. Go shade 3 bricks.

DAY 3
Thinking Day (Interpretation)

1. Pray.

2. Read. Read Psalms 139–142.

3. Reread text. Read 139.

4. Sentence. Expand yesterday's phrase to a sentence:

_____
_____

Journal *Continued*

UPGRADE: Water Hauler
*(color **3 bricks** per day)*

A promotion, eh? Well, at least you'll have plenty to drink while you're working.

Good work. Keep it up.

Hey, you spilled a drop . . .

A Daily and Weekly Devotional

Journal *Daily add things you are thankful for, thoughts about God, and anything else.*

5. Question. If that sentence could be turned into a question, what word could be used (who, what, where, when, why, how)? Rewrite the sentence in the form of a question:

6. Answer(s). Write the answers to your question below. These answers are all the ideas taken from the text.

7. It's #BIBSwall time. Go color in three bricks.

DAY 4
Application Day

1. Pray.

2. Read. Read Psalm 139.

3. Combine. Try to combine the "Trunk" (sentence/question) and the "Branches" (answers) into a complete thought here:

4. Apply. The BIG IDEA you just wrote is what God said. And that's what He's still saying. So now... what is He saying to you?

First, write some general things you learned:

Next, whether you learned it from one word, the big idea, or even some random, obscure thought you had, write any other application you can think of:

5. Plan. Write your plan to DO something different in your life because of what you have learned.

So that I am not deceived, I plan to:

_____
_____
_____
_____

6. Super! Is that . . . Is that a complete row I see? Color three more bricks to see if you can complete one row all the way across.

DAY 5
Reading Day

1. Pray.

2. Read. Read Psalms 146–150.

3. Reread text. Read Psalm 150.

4. Word. What word generally describes this text?

_____

5. Phrase. Now what about that word? Expand it to a phrase:

_____

6. Little by little. You're on a roll! Color three bricks.

RANDOMNOPOLOUSOPOLY. What phrase does this represent?

```
┌─────────────────────┐
│       I     I       │
│     BAG   BAG       │
└─────────────────────┘
```

DAY 6
Thinking Day (Interpretation)

1. Pray.

2. Read. Read Psalms 145–147.

Journal *Continued*

Journal *Daily add things you are thankful for, thoughts about God, and anything else.*

___

3. Reread text. Read Psalm 150.

4. Sentence. Now expand yesterday's phrase to a sentence:

___

5. Question. If that sentence could be turned into a question, what word could be used (who, what, where, when, why, how)? Rewrite the sentence in the form of a question:

___

6. Answer(s). Write the many answers to your question below. These answers are all the ideas taken from the text.

___

7. Almost done with Psalms. Well, not the whole book, but you know what I mean. Go shade in three more bricks.

DAY 7
Application Day

1. Pray.

2. Read. Read Psalm 150.

3. Combine. Try to combine the "Trunk" and the "Branches" into a complete thought here (like Day 4):

___

4. Apply. The BIG IDEA you just wrote is what God said. And that's what He's still saying. So now... what is He saying <u>to you</u>?

First, write some general things you learned.

___

34   B.I.B.S. - Big Idea Bible Study

Next, whether you learned it from one word, the big idea, or even some random, obscure thought you had, write any other application you can think of:

_____

_____

_____

_____

5. Plan. Write your plan to DO something different in your life because of what you have learned.

So that I am not deceived, I plan to:

_____

_____

_____

_____

6. Two monster thumbs up. Well, you're soaked from water (and sweat) from all your hard work, but you have earned the respect of everyone around you. Great work. Go shade in THREE more bricks.

7. JOURNAL REVIEW. Review last week's journal and think about what you might change in the upcoming week (see page 8 for more journaling ideas).

RANDOMNOPOLOUSOPOLY ANSWER (from Day 5): Bags under your eyes

Journal *Continued*

_____

_____

_____

_____

_____

_____

_____

_____

_____

_____

_____

_____

_____

_____

_____

_____

_____

_____

_____

_____

_____

_____

_____

_____

_____

_____

_____

_____

Journal *Daily add things you are thankful for, thoughts about God, and anything else.*

_____
_____
_____
_____
_____
_____
_____
_____
_____
_____
_____
_____
_____
_____

EPHESIANS
WEEK 4

The Apostle Paul won people to Christ and established churches everywhere he went, and the church at Ephesus was thriving. Paul was in his mid-60's when he wrote this letter to encourage the church. It's message is the Gospel—Good News!

In your reading, you will realize that the Gospel breaks down racial and cultural barriers, and makes us into completely new people. It changes us from the inside out, and should affect every area of our lives.

 DAY 1
Reading Day (Observation)

1. Pray. Open in prayer. Ask God's forgiveness for known sin and ask for His help in today's study.

2. Background. If you have a study tool (online source, study Bible, computer software, commentary...), read some background on the book. Write some things you learned here (see p. 12 andAppendix 3 for some ideas.):

_____
_____
_____
_____
_____
_____

3. Read Ephesians. Read the whole book, or set a time limit and read as much as you can in that time to get the overall concept.

4. Note the text divisions. See what's coming up this week. Write the two texts you'll be studying below:

_____

5. You've been UPGRADED. You know what that means... The big bosses have noticed your good work, and they're impressed. They think it's time you get some help. You now have your own little crew, because you've been promoted to BOSS! With your helpers, you get to shade FIVE BRICKS per day. Whoa.

PROMOTION! You're a BOSS.
(color 5 brick per day)

You know the ropes. You've prepped the ground, carved the rock, laid the stones and mixed the mortar. It's time you get a little help.

The big bosses like your work, so they decided to give you your own little crew.

Treat them well. Lead by example. Your hard work is paying off. Keep it up.

36   B.I.B.S. - Big Idea Bible Study

DAY 2
Rereading Day

1. Pray.

2. Read. Read Acts 18–19.

3. Reread text. Read Ephesians 4:11–16.

4. Word. What word generally describes this text (4:11–16)?

_____

5. Phrase. Now what about that word? Expand it to a phrase:

_____

6. Guess what… you've completed almost a month of devotions. That's pretty awesome. And your #BIBSwall is looking pretty great, too. Go color five (5) more bricks.

DAY 3
Thinking Day (Interpretation)

1. Pray.

2. Read. Read Ephesians 3–4.

3. Reread text. Read Ephesians 4:11–16.

4. Sentence. Expand yesterday's phrase to a sentence:

_____
_____

5. Question. If that sentence could be turned into a question, what word could be used (who, what, where, when, why, how)? Rewrite the sentence in the form of a question:

_____
_____

6. Answer(s). Write the answers to your question below. These answers are all the ideas taken from the text.

_____
_____
_____

7. It's #BIBSwall time. Go color in five bricks.

Journal _Continued_

A Daily and Weekly Devotional 37

Journal *Daily add things you are thankful for, thoughts about God, and anything else.*

DAY 4
Application Day

1. Pray.

2. Read. Read Ephesians 4.

3. Combine. Try to combine the "Trunk" (sentence/question) and the "Branches" (answers) into a complete thought here:

_____
_____

4. Apply. The BIG IDEA you just wrote is what God said. And that's what He's still saying. So now... what is He saying <u>to you</u>?

First, write some general things you learned:

_____
_____
_____
_____
_____

Next, whether you learned it from one word, the big idea, or even some random, obscure thought you had, write any other application you can think of:

_____
_____
_____
_____
_____

5. Plan. Write your plan to DO something different in your life because of what you have learned.

So that I am not deceived, I plan to:

_____
_____
_____
_____

6. Convicted? Go blow off some steam by adding five bricks!

B.I.B.S. - Big Idea Bible Study

DAY 5
Rereading Day

1. Pray.

2. Read. Read Ephesians 3–5.

3. Reread text. Read Ephesians 4:17–24.

4. Word. What word generally describes this text (4:17–24)?

_____

5. Phrase. Now what about that word? Expand it to a phrase:

_____

6. Your crew is happy. You're a good boss. Keep it up. Today earned you five more bricks.

RANDOMNOPOLOUSOPOLY: What slogans are represented? (use the first letter of each word) (wait until Day 7 for answer)

Inhabiting **F**loor, **A**n **I**nvalid **C**alls **G**uys **U**rgently (LifeAlert)
Weather's **I**rrelevant **R**egarding **I**odized **P**reservative (Morton Salt)
Jordan's **D**irect **I**nstruction (Nike)

*Adapted from Crowd Pleasing Puzzles book by Patrick Berry and Todd McClary

DAY 6
Thinking Day (Interpretation)

1. Pray.

2. Read. Read Ephesians 1–2.

3. Reread text. Read Ephesians 4:17–24.

4. Sentence. Now expand yesterday's phrase to a sentence:

_____

5. Question. If that sentence could be turned into a question, circle the word that could be used (who, what, where, when, why, how).

Now rewrite the sentence in the form of a question:

_____

Journal Continued

A Daily and Weekly Devotional   39

Journal *Daily add things you are thankful for, thoughts about God, and anything else.*

6. Answer(s). Write the many answers to your question below. These answers are all the ideas taken from the text.

7. Closing in on FOUR weeks. Amazing. Five more bricks!

DAY 7
Application Day

1. Pray.

2. Read. Read Ephesians 4.

3. Combine. Try to combine the "Trunk" and the "Branches" into a complete thought here (like Day 4):

4. Apply. The BIG IDEA you just wrote is what God said. And that's what He's still saying. So now… what is He saying <u>to you</u>?

First, write some general things you learned.

Next, whether you learned it from one word, the big idea, or even some random, obscure thought you had, write any other application you can think of:

5. Plan. Write your plan to DO something different in your life because of what you have learned.

So that I am not deceived, I plan to:

6. This is truly momentous. You just finished a month of devotions. How many Americans can say that? Not many. But you can. Phenomenal. Go add five more bricks to your wall!

7. JOURNAL REVIEW. Close this week out by thinking about how GOOD God has been to you.

RANDOMNOPOLOUSOPOLY ANSWER (from Day 5):
I've Fallen And I Can't Get Up
When It Rains, It Pours
Just Do It

EPHESIANS (CONTINUED)
WEEK 5

DAY 1
Reading Day (Observation)

1. Pray. Open in prayer. Ask God's forgiveness for known sin and ask for His help in today's study.

2. Background. If you have a study tool (online source, study Bible, computer software, commentary...), read some more background on the book. Write some things you learned here (see p. 12 and Appendix 3 for some ideas.):

_____
_____
_____
_____

3. Read more background. Read Acts 19–20.

4. Note the text divisions. See what's coming up this week. Write the two texts you'll be studying below:

_____

5. Keep after 'em, boss. Promotions aren't doled out like they used to be. Oh well. Keep after it; your time will come.

Fun fact: Imagine a bird transferring the earth—one mouthful at a time—to the moon. Long time? Eternity hasn't even started yet.

Journal *Continued*

Journal *Daily add things you are thankful for, thoughts about God, and anything else.*

_____
_____
_____
_____
_____
_____
_____
_____
_____
_____
_____
_____
_____
_____
_____
_____
_____
_____
_____
_____
_____
_____
_____
_____
_____
_____
_____

DAY 2
Rereading Day

1. Pray.

2. Read. Read Ephesians 4–5.

3. Reread text. Read Ephesians 5:1–4.

4. Word. What word generally describes this text (5:1–4)?

_____

5. Phrase. Now what about that word? Expand it to a phrase:

_____
_____

6. And . . . Cut! One more day. Five more bricks.

DAY 3
Thinking Day (Interpretation)

1. Pray.

2. Read. Read Ephesians 5–6.

3. Reread text. Read Ephesians 5:1–4.

4. Sentence. Expand yesterday's phrase to a sentence:

_____
_____

5. Question. If that sentence could be turned into a question, what word could be used (who, what, where, when, why, how)? Rewrite the sentence in the form of a question:

_____
_____

6. Answer(s). Write the answers to your question below. These answers are all the ideas taken from the text.

_____
_____
_____

7. #BIBSwall time. Don't forget to post a pic! Five more bricks.

DAY 4
Application Day

1. Pray.

2. Read. Read Ephesians 5.

3. Combine. Try to combine the "Trunk" (sentence/question) and the "Branches" (answers) into a complete thought here:

_____
_____

4. Apply. The BIG IDEA you just wrote is what God said. And that's what He's still saying. So now... what is He saying <u>to you</u>?

First, write some general things you learned:

_____
_____
_____
_____

Next, whether you learned it from one word, the big idea, or even some random, obscure thought you had, write any other application you can think of:

_____
_____
_____
_____

5. Plan. Write your plan to DO something different in your life because of what you have learned.

So that I am not deceived, I plan to:

_____
_____
_____
_____

6. Color time. Like Kindergarten. Aww... Color five bricks!

Journal *Continued*

A Daily and Weekly Devotional 43

Journal *Daily add things you are thankful for, thoughts about God, and anything else.*

DAY 5
Reading Day

1. Pray.

2. Read. Read Ephesians 4–6.

3. Reread text. Read Ephesians 5:19–21.

4. Word. What word generally describes this text (5:19–21)?

_____

5. Phrase. Now what about that word? Expand it to a phrase:

_____
_____

6. You're a boss! Both literally and colloquially. Five bricks.

RANDOMNOPOLOUSOPOLY. What phrases do these represent?

| POLMOMICE | ROOD |

DAY 6
Thinking Day (Interpretation)

1. Pray.

2. Read. Read Ephesians 1–2.

3. Reread text. Read Ephesians 5:19–21.

4. Sentence. Now expand yesterday's phrase to a sentence:

_____
_____

5. Question. If that sentence could be turned into a question, what word could be used (who, what, where, when, why, how)? Rewrite the sentence in the form of a question:

_____
_____

6. Answer(s). Write the many answers to your question below. These answers are all the ideas taken from the text.

_____
_____
_____

7. Wall? Check. Five bricks, here we come!

DAY 7
Application Day

1. Pray.

2. Read. Read Ephesians 5.

3. Combine. Try to combine the "Trunk" and the "Branches" into a complete thought here (like Day 4):

_____
_____
_____

4. Apply. The BIG IDEA you just wrote is what God said. And that's what He's still saying. So now… what is He saying to you?

First, write some general things you learned.

_____
_____
_____
_____
_____

Next, whether you learned it from one word, the big idea, or even some random, obscure thought you had, write any other application you can think of:

_____
_____
_____
_____
_____

Journal *Continued*

Journal *Daily add things you are thankful for, thoughts about God, and anything else.*

_____
_____
_____
_____
_____
_____
_____
_____
_____
_____
_____
_____
_____
_____
_____
_____
_____

**YOU'VE GROWN SMARTER:
Engineer**
(color 6 bricks per day)

Your crew was struggling to bucket the water in, mix and spread the mortar, and set the stones, so you took matters into your own hands.

When the big bosses saw your canals to bring in water and the crane to lift the rocks... I mean, WOW. A crane? Yep. You're going places.

5. Plan. Write your plan to DO something different in your life because of what you have learned.

So that I am not deceived, I plan to:

_____
_____
_____
_____
_____
_____
_____

6. Zowie . . . Boss, you're an inspiration. This wall has never looked so good. Your work has been inspirational. Five more!

7. JOURNAL REVIEW. Hey... don't skip this step! (Stopped journaling? See page 8 for ideas for next week.)

RANDOMNOPOLOUSOPOLY ANSWER (from Day 5): Mother-in-law ("mom" in "police"): Back Door.

EPHESIANS (CONTINUED)
WEEK 6

DAY 1
Reading Day (Observation)

1. Pray. Open in prayer. Ask God's forgiveness for known sin and ask for His help in today's study.

2. Background. Read some more background on the book or on the upcoming chapters. Write some things you learned here (see p. 12 and Appendix 3 for some ideas.):

_____
_____
_____
_____
_____

3. Get the context. Review Acts 18–20.

46 B.I.B.S. - Big Idea Bible Study

4. Note the text divisions. See what's coming up this week. Write the two texts you'll be studying below:

_____

5. YOU'VE GROWN SMARTER. Boy, promotions take a while these days, huh? It's been two weeks, but you've used your time to learn and improve your crew. You engineered a canal system to haul water AND a crane to lift the rocks. Your work is improving everyone's lives, and you can now do SIX bricks per day.

Fun fact: pick up a handful of sand and count the grains. Each speck counts as a thought God has toward you! (139:17–18)

DAY 2
Rereading Day

1. Pray.

2. Read. Read Ephesians 5–6.

3. Reread text. Read Ephesians 6:1–3.

4. Word. What word generally describes this text (6:1–3)?

_____

5. Phrase. Now what about that word? Expand it to a phrase:

_____

_____

6. I'm so proud. . . An engineer? Like an inventor? Six bricks for you.

DAY 3
Thinking Day (Interpretation)

1. Pray.

2. Read. Read Ephesians 4–5.

3. Reread text. Read Ephesians 6:1–3.

4. Sentence. Expand yesterday's phrase to a sentence:

_____

_____

Journal *Continued*

Journal *Daily add things you are thankful for, thoughts about God, and anything else.*

_____
_____
_____
_____
_____
_____
_____
_____
_____
_____
_____
_____
_____
_____
_____
_____
_____
_____
_____
_____
_____
_____
_____
_____

5. Question. If that sentence could be turned into a question, what word could be used (who, what, where, when, why, how)? Rewrite the sentence in the form of a question:

_____
_____

6. Answer(s). Write the answers to your question below. These answers are all the ideas taken from the text.

_____
_____
_____

7. It's #BIBSwall time. Go color in six bricks.

DAY 4
Application Day

1. Pray.

2. Read. Read Ephesians 6.

3. Combine. Try to combine the "Trunk" (sentence/question) and the "Branches" (answers) into a complete thought here:

_____
_____

4. Apply. The BIG IDEA you just wrote is what God said. And that's what He's still saying. So now... what is He saying <u>to you</u>?

First, write some general things you learned:

_____
_____
_____
_____

Next, whether you learned it from one word, the big idea, or even some random, obscure thought you had, write any other application you can think of:

_____
_____
_____
_____

5. Plan. Write your plan to DO something different in your life because of what you have learned.

So that I am not deceived, I plan to:

_____
_____
_____
_____

6. Some wall! It's not the Great Wall of China, but it's getting close. Six more bricks.

DAY 5
Reading Day

1. Pray.

2. Read. Read Ephesians 3–5.

3. Reread text. Read Ephesians 6:10–17.

4. Word. What word generally describes this text (6:10–17)?

_____

5. Phrase. Now what about that word? Expand it to a phrase:

_____

6. Build the wall! Finish the week strong. Color six bricks.

RANDOMNOPOLOUSOPOLY. What phrases do these represent?

| Mil1ion | y
n
n
u
s |

DAY 6
Thinking Day (Interpretation)

1. Pray.

Journal *Continued*

A Daily and Weekly Devotional   49

Journal *Daily add things you are thankful for, thoughts about God, and anything else.*

_____
_____
_____
_____
_____
_____
_____
_____
_____
_____
_____
_____
_____
_____
_____
_____
_____
_____
_____
_____
_____
_____
_____
_____
_____
_____

2. Read. Read Ephesians 5–6

3. Reread text. Read Ephesians 6:10–17.

4. Sentence. Now expand yesterday's phrase to a sentence:

_____
_____

5. Question. If that sentence could be turned into a question, what word could be used (who, what, where, when, why, how)? Rewrite the sentence in the form of a question:

_____
_____

6. Answer(s). Write the many answers to your question below. These answers are all the ideas taken from the text.

_____
_____
_____

7. Only one more day. Ephesians has been amazing, kind of like your wall! Go add six more bricks.

DAY 7
Application Day

1. Pray.

2. Read. Read Ephesians 6.

3. Combine. Try to combine the "Trunk" and the "Branches" into a complete thought here (like Day 4):

_____
_____
_____

4. Apply. The BIG IDEA you just wrote is what God said. And that's what He's still saying. So now… what is He saying <u>to you</u>?

First, write some general things you learned.

_____
_____
_____
_____

Next, whether you learned it from one word, the big idea, or even some random, obscure thought you had, write any other application you can think of:

_____
_____
_____
_____

5. Plan. Write your plan to DO something different in your life because of what you have learned.

So that I am not deceived, I plan to:

_____
_____
_____
_____
_____

6. This is it. Six weeks. Boom. Done. Three books of the Bible . . . Boom. Done. Philemon, Psalms, and now Ephesians. At this rate, you'll be a scholar in no time.

For now, though, you're still an engineer. Keep it up for another week. Six more bricks earned today!

7. JOURNAL REVIEW. Read over your journal. Ain't God good? (see page 8 for more journaling ideas for next week)

RANDOMNOPOLOUSOPOLY ANSWER (from Day 5): One in a million; sunny side up.

Journal *Continued*

NEHEMIAH
WEEK 7

🕐 A LITTLE CHANGE...
Journaling Days

Narrative. I have found that the narrative format is a little harder to put through the strict BIBS process. Narrative is more of a story than a single principle. Although I still believe there can be only one interpretation, this section will focus on the humans in these scenes and how they responded to God.

As you read Nehemiah, think of yourself in their situation. Each day will be more of a journaling layout rather than the Word>Phrase>Sentence>Question>etc. layout. Use the **prompt questions** to get your mind going in their world. **You don't have to answer ALL the questions or ONLY the questions.** They are a guide to show you what journaling can be.

Enjoy!

-RR

Most of the history of Nehemiah is included in the book itself. While Ezra was a spiritual leader of Israel, Nehemiah was more of a politician or a business leader. He had a crucial role in rallying the people to rebuild the walls of Jerusalem, showing God's faithfulness to His covenant people.

The events of the book are some of the last events recorded in the Old Testament. Babylon had destroyed Israel and the Jews had been in captivity for 70 years. Around the end of Daniel's life, several waves of Jews were allowed to return home to Jerusalem, while others had lived there all the time with broken walls. They were a defeated people–politically and emotionally.

Nehemiah's burden was to go home (to Jerusalem) and return God's land to its intended glory. It's not the BIBS wall, but it's close. (See the connection now?)

DAY 1
Reading Day (Observation)

1. Pray. Open in prayer. Ask God's forgiveness for known sin and ask for His help in today's study.

2. Background. If you have a study tool (online source, study Bible, computer software, commentary…), read some background on the book. Write some things you learned here (see p. 12 and Appendix 3 for some ideas.):

_____
_____
_____

3. Read Nehemiah. Read the whole book, or set a time limit and read as much as you can in that time to get a big picture.

4. Look ahead. What chapters will you cover this week?

_____

5. Keep up the good work. Wow! You are a super-engineer. That's not a promotion . . . but people are calling you super! Your "Claw" machine is wow-ing everybody with the stones it can lift. Impressive! You are destined for great things . . . (six more bricks!)

DAY 2
Journaling Day

1. Pray.

2. Read. Read Nehemiah 1–3.

3. Reread text. Read Nehemiah 1.

4. Think and write. Use the questions this week as ideas on what to write about:

Think of Nehemiah as a regular guy. Could he be a friend of yours?

Would you say that Nehemiah is the "real deal?"

_____
_____
_____
_____

Journal *Continued*

Journal *Daily add things you are thankful for, thoughts about God, and anything else.*

_____

5. **Engineering genius.** Build, build, build! Six more...

DAY 3
Journaling Day

1. **Pray.**

2. **Read.** Read Nehemiah 1–2.

3. **Reread text.** Read Nehemiah 1.

4. **Think and write.** Use the questions this week as ideas on what to write about:

How emotional do you think he was about his prayer?

_____

5. **Nearing the end.** Observe that wall. It's a thing of beauty.

DAY 4
Application Day

1. **Pray.**

2. **Read.** Read Nehemiah 1.

3. **Apply.**

First, write some general things you learned:

_____

Next, whether you learned it from one word, a big idea, or even some random, obscure thought you had, write any other application you can think of:

_____
_____
_____
_____

4. Plan. Write your plan to DO something different in your life because of what you have learned.

So that I am not deceived, I plan to:

_____
_____
_____
_____

5. Champ. You're making the Bible real. That's what it's all about. Keep it up. Reward yourself by building on the wall. It's almost done!

DAY 5
Journaling Day

1. Pray.

2. Read. Read Nehemiah 1–3.

3. Reread text. Read Nehemiah 2.

4. Think and write. Use the questions this week as ideas on what to write about:

Could you respond like Nehemiah when you're nervous? (Remember, he was talking to a king who could have killed him just for being sad in his presence.)

What kind of BIG vision has God given you?

_____
_____
_____

Journal *Continued*

A Daily and Weekly Devotional 55

Journal *Daily add things you are thankful for, thoughts about God, and anything else.*

5. The fifth day. Nehemiah can help you build your life. And you can help him build his wall. Six more bricks.

RANDOMNOPOLOUSOPOLY: What is the next word in the sequence (wait until Day 7 for answer)?

- Twin / Full / Queen
- Eagle/Birdy/Par
- Kill/Commit Adultery/Steal
- Pacific/Mountain/Central

*Adapted from <u>Crowd Pleasing Puzzles</u> book by Patrick Berry and Todd McClary

DAY 6
Journaling Day

1. Pray.

2. Read. Read Nehemiah 2–3.

3. Reread text. Read Nehemiah 2.

4. Think and write. Use the questions this week as ideas on what to write about:

Was Nehemiah a planner?

Talk about his vision from God:

5. One more week, almost done! I'm impressed. Week after week, you're still after it. Finish this week strong!

56   B.I.B.S. - Big Idea Bible Study

DAY 7
Application Day

1. Pray.

2. Read. Read Nehemiah 2.

3. Apply.

First, write some general things you learned:

_____
_____
_____
_____

Next, whether you learned it from one word, a big idea, or even some random, obscure thought you had, write any other application you can think of:

_____
_____
_____
_____

4. Plan. Write your plan to DO something different in your life because of what you have learned.

So that I am not deceived, I plan to:

_____
_____
_____

5. *Cue BIBS theme music... Hear that? It's your very own theme song... Did John Williams score that for you? Six more brick, coming right up!

6. JOURNAL REVIEW. It's been a new kind of week in the journaling front. How'd you like it?

RANDOMNOPOLOUSOPOLY ANSWER (from Day 5):
King; Bogey; Bear False Witness (Lie); Eastern

Journal *Continued*

A Daily and Weekly Devotional 57

Journal *Daily add things you are thankful for, thoughts about God, and anything else.*

_____
_____
_____
_____
_____
_____
_____
_____
_____
_____
_____
_____
_____
_____

NEHEMIAH (CONTINUED)
WEEK 8

DAY 1
Reading Day (Observation)

1. Pray. Open in prayer. Ask God's forgiveness for known sin and ask for His help in today's study.

2. Background. Read Ezra 1–2 for some more context to Nehemiah. Thoughts?

_____
_____
_____

3. Look ahead. What chapters will you cover this week?

_____

4. There's not too many bosses over you, now. You've proven yourself time and time again. No longer do you report to a whole chain of bosses . . . now the crew leaders report to you.

You've been promoted to OVERSEER. Now you need to coordinate all the comings and goings of every worker everywhere. You up to the challenge? If you keep it up, you'll be able to lay **seven stones per day.** Now that's a work crew.

Public Service Announcement: Tired of forgetting things like homework sheets or gym shorts? Put them over something you know you'll remember (like your phone or shoes).

WE NEED YOUR SKILLS
Overseer
(color 7 bricks per day)

You're too valuable to be doing the labor. You know too much. You've done it all.

It's time you start helping in other ways. We need you to make it all happen. Your new job-should you decide to accept it-is to coordinate this whole project. Can you handle it? I know you can.

DAY 2
Journaling Day

1. Pray.

2. Read. Read Nehemiah 3–5.

3. Reread text. Read Nehemiah 4.

4. Think and write. Write about this week's questions:

58 B.I.B.S. - Big Idea Bible Study

To me, opposition looks like...

Nehemiah ignored the haters. He just prayed. Have you been lied about? How did you react?

_____
_____
_____
_____
_____
_____

5. Good overseeing. People come to you for advice on all topics (mortar, stones, machines...). Since you've had the experience in all these areas, you are making people's lives better by sharing your knowledge. Keep it up! Seven stones laid today.

DAY 3
Journaling Day

1. Pray.

2. Read. Read Nehemiah 3–4.

3. Reread text. Read Nehemiah 4.

4. Think and write. Use the questions this week as ideas on what to write about:

How many godly friends do you have? _____ Nehemiah didn't have many–even his friends were discouraging him. How did Nehemiah respond?

_____
_____
_____
_____
_____
_____

5. The habit is pretty entrenched now. After building for so long, it seems easy now. Reading your Bible can become a lifelong habit if you make it a priority. Good work. Seven more stones.

Journal *Continued*

Journal *Daily add things you are thankful for, thoughts about God, and anything else.*

_____

DAY 4
Application Day

1. Pray.

2. Read. Read Nehemiah 4.

3. Apply.

First, write some general things you learned:

_____

Next, whether you learned it from one word, a big idea, or even some random, obscure thought you had, write any other application you can think of:

_____

4. Plan. Write your plan to DO something different in your life because of what you have learned.

So that I am not deceived, I plan to:

_____

5. Color time. Seven more bricks!

DAY 5
Journaling Day

1. Pray.

2. Read. Read Nehemiah 4–6.

3. Reread text. Read Nehemiah 5.

4. Think and write. Use the questions this week as ideas on what to write about:

60   B.I.B.S. - Big Idea Bible Study

At times, you'll get overwhelmed thinking no one is on your side. Nehemiah did. Even then, describe his response:

_____
_____
_____
_____
_____

5. Start training someone to take your place. The promotions don't last long around here. I'm seeing another new assignment in your future. Today, though, seven more bricks.

RANDOMNOPOLOUSOPOLY. *What phrases do these represent?*

12"	m ce
12"	m ce
	m ce

DAY 6
Journaling Day

1. Pray.

2. Read. Read Nehemiah 5–7.

3. Reread text. Read Nehemiah 5.

4. Think and write. Use the questions this week as ideas on what to write about:

What is your typical response to conflict?

_____
_____
_____
_____
_____

5. Great work. Post your #BIBSwall to social media and show the progress. Seven more bricks.

Journal *Daily add things you are thankful for, thoughts about God, and anything else.*

_____
_____
_____
_____
_____
_____
_____
_____
_____
_____
_____
_____
_____
_____
_____
_____
_____
_____
_____
_____
_____
_____
_____
_____
_____

DAY 7
Application Day

1. Pray.

2. Read. Read Nehemiah 5.

3. Apply.

First, write some general things you learned:

_____
_____
_____
_____
_____

Next, whether you learned it from one word, a big idea, or even some random, obscure thought you had, write any other application you can think of:

_____
_____
_____
_____
_____
_____

4. Plan. Write your plan to DO something different in your life because of what you have learned.

So that I am not deceived, I plan to:

_____
_____
_____
_____

5. Your wall is monstrous! Phew! These rows are flying up, now. You might even have to draw in your own bricks if you keep this up.

6. JOURNAL REVIEW. The point of the journal is to help you. Your goal is not some "right answer." You're trying to impress exactly no one. So, make the most of it next week!

RANDOMNOPOLOUSOPOLY ANSWER (from Day 5): Two left feet (12 inches); Three Blind Mice (3 "Mice" with no "i"s, or, eyes.)

62   B.I.B.S. - Big Idea Bible Study

NEHEMIAH (CONTINUED)
WEEK 9

DAY 1
Reading Day (Observation)

1. Pray. Open in prayer. Ask God's forgiveness for known sin and ask for His help in today's study.

2. Background. Read Ezra 3–6 for more context to Nehemiah's story. Thoughts?

___

3. Look ahead. What chapters will you cover this week?

___

4. "I'm sending you on a little trip . . ." You thought they'd never ask. The only thing holding you back now is information. You don't know what you don't know. So you need to go out, do some research, and find out more efficient solutions to problems you did not even know existed!

You're on a research quest to uncover more and faster ways to work. Who knows, maybe you'll discover an alien race that you could convince to help you? Maybe not...

Oh... **eight bricks,** please.

Fun fact: even though you think he's weird, that "one guy" in your class is actually not an alien. Fact. Can't prove it wrong.

DAY 2
Journaling Day

1. Pray.

2. Read. Read Nehemiah 5–7.

3. Reread text. Read Nehemiah 6.

4. Think and write. Use the questions this week as ideas on what to write about:

Journal *Continued*

___

JOURNEY TO... Explorer
*(color **8 bricks** per day)*

You've tapped the limits of the education systems here—you've learned everything there is to know. But you know there's more out there.

You set off for new lands, experiences, and abilities that you never knew existed. Maybe someone out there knows something you don't know about wall-building. Surely.

Journal *Daily add things you are thankful for, thoughts about God, and anything else.*

More lies. What if Nehemiah had stopped?

5. Keep it up. Eight more bricks for you.

DAY 3
Journaling Day

1. Pray.

2. Read. Read Nehemiah 6–7.

3. Reread text. Read Nehemiah 6.

4. Think and write. Use the questions this week as ideas on what to write about:

What in the world could you learn from Chapter 7?

5. No aliens yet. You haven't found any alien species yet, but your journey HAS helped you build better walls. Eight more…

DAY 4
Application Day

1. Pray.

2. Read. Read Nehemiah 6.

3. Apply.

First, write some general things you learned:

_____
_____
_____

Next, whether you learned it from one word, a big idea, or even some random, obscure thought you had, write any other application you can think of:

_____
_____
_____

4. Plan. Write your plan to DO something different in your life because of what you have learned.

So that I am not deceived, I plan to:

_____
_____
_____

5. Okay! Just a few more bricks…

DAY 5
Journaling Day

1. Pray.

2. Read. Read Nehemiah 7–10.

3. Reread text. Read Nehemiah 8.

4. Think and write. Use the questions this week as ideas on what to write about:

The people were hungry for God's Word. Articulate your hunger for God.

_____
_____
_____

Journal *Continued*

_____
_____
_____
_____
_____
_____
_____
_____
_____
_____
_____
_____
_____
_____
_____
_____
_____
_____
_____
_____
_____
_____
_____
_____
_____
_____
_____
_____
_____
_____

Journal *Daily add things you are thankful for, thoughts about God, and anything else.*

5. What's the Hebrew word for amazing, 'cuz that's you. Well... That's your wall, anyway. Eight more bricks.

RANDOMNOPOLOUSOPOLY*. What phrases do these represent?*

NHAPPY	**SCISAB** **SCISAB**
F O DRACULA	give get (×4)

DAY 6
Journaling Day

1. Pray.

2. Read. Read Nehemiah 8–9.

3. Reread text. Read Nehemiah 8.

4. Think and write. Use the questions this week as ideas on what to write about:

As soon as they understood, they obeyed. Do you do that? What can you change?

5. Nearly another week. This thing is flying now! Eight more.

DAY 7
Application Day

1. Pray.

2. Read. Read Nehemiah 8.

3. Apply.

First, write some general things you learned:

_____
_____
_____
_____
_____
_____

Next, whether you learned it from one word, a big idea, or even some random, obscure thought you had, write any other application you can think of:

_____
_____
_____
_____
_____
_____

4. Plan. Write your plan to DO something different in your life because of what you have learned.

So that I am not deceived, I plan to:

_____
_____
_____
_____
_____

5. Whamo. No one saw this coming. It has been just over 60 days, and this wall is lookin' good! Eight more bricks!

6. JOURNAL REVIEW. Read over your journal. There's a bit more to review, huh?

Journal *Continued*

Journal *Daily add things you are thankful for, thoughts about God, and anything else.*

_____
_____
_____
_____
_____
_____
_____
_____
_____
_____
_____
_____

VISIONARY
*(color **10 bricks** per day)*

They always said, "Keep your eye on the prize." You thought the prize would be the wall, or the glory of being the leader, or the fame of making it all happen.

You realize that's not it at all.

The prize is the journey itself; not the destination. The prize is the people you've helped. The prize is the product that goes on to outlive you.

The prize is God's pleasure.

Boy . . . This is even better than you could have ever imagined!

God, thank you for letting me be a part of something GREAT. What do you have next for me?

68   B.I.B.S. - Big Idea Bible Study

RANDOMNOPOLOUSOPOLY ANSWER (from Day 5): Unhappy without you (U); Back to ("two") basics; Down for the Count [Dracula]; Forgive and Forget (4 give; 4 get).

NEHEMIAH (CONTINUED)
WEEK 10

DAY 1
Reading Day (Observation)

1. Pray. Open in prayer. Ask God's forgiveness for known sin and ask for His help in today's study.

2. Background. Read Ezra 7–10 for Ezra's perspective on the city of Jerusalem in Nehemiah's day. Thoughts?

_____
_____
_____
_____

3. Look ahead. What chapters will you cover this week?

_____

4. YOU'VE DONE IT. Putting others ahead of yourself has brought you to this moment in time: The Final Week. As you close the project down and look up at your wall, you can't help but be overwhelmed at the amazing efforts of so many people.

No, this isn't your wall, after all. This is something that GOD built. This is something GREAT. This is bigger than you.

Sure, others might credit you for being a "VISIONARY," but you know you wouldn't be here if it weren't for a lot of others in your life, pushing you forward and helping you through. Most of all, you realize that any vision worth while can only be from God and for God.

The #BIBSwall might feel like your creation, but it's a masterpiece of God's doing. Bible reading, too, might feel like a personal accomplishment (if you have been faithful at it thus far), but it's really just God working IN and THROUGH you that makes the difference.

God is SO good to allow us to be used in mighty ways. Only when we realize it is NOT about us can we fully bask in the beauty of a job well done.

This week is your last. Your grand vision has paid off. God is pleased.

Now, shade in **10 bricks per day.** You've earned it.

DAY 2
Journaling Day

1. Pray.

2. Read. Read Nehemiah 7–9.

3. Reread text. Read Nehemiah 9.

4. Think and write. Use the questions this week as ideas on what to write about:

The people were serious and emotional. Describe the last time God moved in your life like that…

5. Plan now… What's after this BIBS book? How will you continue? (Shade 10 bricks)

DAY 3
Journaling Day

1. Pray.

2. Read. Read Nehemiah 8–9.

3. Reread text. Read Nehemiah 9.

Journal *Daily add things you are thankful for, thoughts about God, and anything else.*

4. Think and write. Use the questions this week as ideas on what to write about:

Can you learn anything from Chapters 10–12 (Hint: The answer is "yes")? If so, what?

5. This is the last week, but it's not the end. This week should be a time to plan for next week. What's next in your walk with God? (Shade 10 bricks)

DAY 4
Application Day

1. Pray.

2. Read. Read Nehemiah 9.

3. Apply.

First, write some general things you learned:

Next, whether you learned it from one word, a big idea, or even some random, obscure thought you had, write any other application you can think of:

4. Plan. Write your plan to DO something different in your life because of what you have learned.

So that I am not deceived, I plan to:

___

___

___

5. Just about finished! This wall is getting a little crowded. Just a few final touches. (10 more)

DAY 5
Journaling Day

1. Pray.

2. Read. Read Nehemiah 12–13.

3. Reread text. Read Nehemiah 13.

4. Think and write. Use the questions this week as ideas on what to write about:

When people get right with God they return things to his design. Celebrate God a while. Write some of the things YOU have changed as a result of obeying Him...

___

___

___

___

___

___

5. Being intentional is hard work. But hard work builds walls. You realize that now. Keep it up. Ten more bricks.

Journal *Daily add things you are thankful for, thoughts about God, and anything else.*

___

RANDOMNOPOLOUSOPOLY. *What phrases do these represent?*

| Notic | RAE FAED |

| HOUSE / STOVE | _O_ Ph. D / M. A. / B. A. |

DAY 6
Application Day

1. Pray.

2. Read. Read Nehemiah 13.

3. Apply.

First, write some general things you learned:

___
___
___

Next, whether you learned it from one word, a big idea, or even some random, obscure thought you had, write any other application you can think of:

___
___
___

4. Plan. Write your plan to DO something different in your life because of what you have learned.

So that I am not deceived, I plan to:

___
___

72 B.I.B.S. - Big Idea Bible Study

5. This is it. Man. Sad to see the journey end. That's what happens at the end of big projects, but that's what the next project is for. What will it be for you? Ten more bricks...

DAY 7
Journaling Day

1. Pray.

2. Read. Read Nehemiah 1 & 13.

3. Review the book. Look over Nehemiah as a whole.

4. Think and write.

What has Nehemiah meant to you?

_____
_____
_____
_____
_____
_____
_____

5. Done and done. This book is done. This wall is done.

I'm so happy for you. God is pleased.

Keep up the good work.

Now that this BIBS book is done, I plan to:

_____
_____
_____
_____

RANDOMNOPOLOUSOPOLY ANSWER (from Day 5): Short notice; Turn a deaf ear; Home on the range (stove); Three degrees below zero (college degrees).

Journal *Continued*

A Daily and Weekly Devotional 73

APPENDIX 1 – Sources for Ideas

The ideas for the structure, layout and format of this devotional book are derived from several different sources, although the exact structure is unique as what we are calling our BIBS model. Although our church does not necessarily agree with every aspect of each of these authors' teachings, ideas were taken from the following:

- ***My Biography of God*, by Sam Brock.** *My Biography of God* is a daily devotional set up in a one-week format. Each week the reader studies a certain passage every day and answers questions from the text that lead him to conclusions about God. The conclusions are written in various formats throughout the book, including attributes about God, names of God and more. *My Biography of God* is produced by *Iron Sharpeneth Iron*—the publication ministry of Ironwood Christian Camp.
- ***Living by the Book*, by Howard Hendricks.** *Living by the Book* is a book divided into clear sections emphasizing various Bible study techniques. The main idea borrowed from this book was that Bible study should be done in a sequence of observation, interpretation and application.
- ***How to Read the Bible for All Its Worth*, by Gordon Fee and Douglas Stewart.** *How to...* is an instructional book on interpreting various biblical genres.
- ***Biblical Preaching*, by Haddon Robinson.** *Biblical Preaching* is an instructional book on how to study the Bible in order to present a single concept (big idea) through preaching. Many examples in the BIBS explanations and appendices are taken from *Biblical Preaching*. Further examples included are the concepts about the subject and complement.
- ***Invitation to Biblical Preaching*, by Don Sunukjian.** *Invitation to Biblical Preaching* is an instructional book on how to study the Bible in order to present a single concept (big idea) through preaching. The main wording borrowed for the BIBS format are the questions: "What is God saying?" (big idea) and "What is God saying *to us*?" (application)

APPENDIX 2 – BIBS: Big Idea Bible Study

BIBS
Big Idea Bible Study

BIBS is a suite of devotionals taking the student through many books of the Bible. While each devotional includes its own directions on what to fill out each day, the instructional book (pictured left) was designed to be the in-depth description of each step.

BIBS: Big Idea Bible Study (not to be confused with this *BIBS Devotional*) answers the three main questions of Bible study and provides a format on which to build. The three questions are WHY do we study the Bible, HOW should we study it, and WHAT should we do with it?

The *BIBS* devotionals are all-inclusive and self explanatory, but the book *BIBS: Big Idea Bible Study* provides a richer explanation of the BIBS process.

For more information on ordering, please contact Calvary Baptist Publications at (951) 676-8700, or find them on <u>Amazon.com</u>.

APPENDIX 3 - Examples

EXAMPLE 1 - PSALM 117

1. O praise the Lord, all ye nations: praise him, all ye people.

2. For his merciful kindness is great toward us: and the truth of the Lord endureth for ever. Praise ye the Lord.

OBSERVATION

We know very little about the Psalm itself, but because it's a Psalm we understand that it is probably to God or about God.

INTERPRETATION

Read and reread the text. Done. Didn't take long.

Flag words. I understand all the words, but looking up certain words adds depth to my understanding.

V2 – Great – Prevail. Have strength. Mighty. Confirm, give strength.

V2 – Endureth for ever. Everlasting. Eternal. Unending future.

Word. Praise

Phrase. Praise the Lord

Sentence. We should praise the Lord.

Question Word. Why?

Question. Why should we praise the Lord?

Answers: 1) His merciful kindness and 2) His truth endures.

Big Idea. We should praise the Lord because His mercy is great toward us and His truth endures forever.

APPLICATION

First, God is merciful to me. Why does He choose to be merciful? Why does He have to be merciful? What is He merciful toward? Why would He be called merciful? If He's merciful, that must mean that He is holding back some kind of wrath or punishment.

I certainly deserve a lot of punishment for my sin. I know my own heart; my own lusts. I know what I'm like when no one is around. And... wow... God shows mercy to me every day. What an amazing God! He is so longsuffering with my sin, and He allows me the chance to repent and forsake my sin. God, thank you for showing mercy.

Second, His kindness. God not only does NOT give me punishment when I deserve it, but he DOES give me things that I do not deserve.

Thank you, God, for being so merciful to me. Thank you, on top of that, for being kind and giving me so much. I don't deserve my healthy body, but You are kind enough to give it to me. I have a great family, parents who love me, a loving church to attend, friends who want to help me, I live in America and I'm spoiled rotten with all the conveniences you give me. Thank you, God.

Third, You're not only merciful and kind, but those qualities are GREAT toward me! Why would you offer me mercy even once? And why in the world do You KEEP being merciful and kind even when you know my heart?! You have heaped on the blessings over and over, and I never really thank you properly for it.

The second "branch" was about your truth. I was allowed to read Your very words to me. I can know that there's something true in my life because Your Word has never been proven wrong. It is Truth. And it's still around. And no matter how many people have tried and will try to attack it, it still endures. It's forever! It's eternal. No other book is like that. Thank you, God, that I can know Your Truth!

All this, God... Your merciful kindness that is GREAT toward me... and Your wonderful Truth that you allow me to know and study. How can I keep silent about you?! You're SO good to me! And I too often fail You. Forgive me, God. But more than that, I PRAISE you! Praise God for being SO good to me! Thank you God! I want to serve You more and MORE every day!

MY PLAN: So that I am not deceived, I plan to attend church this Sunday morning and night and REALLY take part in the praise portion of our services. I'm going to sing loud, concentrate on the words, have a heart of gratitude and let is show on my face this Sunday. Hopefully everyone will be able to tell this praise is finally real with me.

Why Read the Bible?

Not only is reading and studying the Bible a GOOD idea, it's GOD'S idea.

If you can read the Scripture with an open heart, God will reveal SO much to you, including Himself, His will, His Son, His goodness, and so much more. Reading the Bible should not be approached as something you MUST do, but as something you're privileged to do.

Think of false religions. They serve gods that they don't even know—gods that are fickle, feeble, or selfish. Worshipers are never quite sure how they can appease their gods, so they offer a sacrifice and hope it is enough. When the weather changes, for example, they don't know why, and it causes fear.

Why?

Because they do not know their gods.

But our God—THE God—has revealed Himself to us through His Word.

Some object, "But what about other religious books?" Their books are simple collections of man's sayings. They are filled with errors and confusion. They do not even claim to be the full revelation of the gods, like the Bible claims to be about God.

When we read the Bible, it's as if we are taking a look into Jesus Himself, who is God: "In the beginning was the Word, and the Word was with God, and the Word was God... And the Word was made flesh, and dwelt among us, (and we beheld his glory, the glory as of the only begotten of the Father,) full of grace and truth." (John 1:1, 14)

We read what we want to know. It makes sense as Christians to want to know God fully, so any devoted Christian will be a student of God's Word.

Why read the Bible?

IT'S GOD'S IDEA

IT IS COMMANDED

» While this is not technically a *direct* command to you and me, in the mind of God, one of his ideals for seeing God's people return to Him was to seek His word:

- Isaiah 34:16 - Seek ye out the book of the Lord and read...

» God told the king to write his own copy out and read it:

- Deut. 17:18-20 And it shall be, when he sitteth upon the throne of his kingdom, that he shall write him a copy of this law in a book out of that which is before the priests the Levites: And it shall be with him, and he shall read therein all the days of his life: that he may learn to fear the LORD his God, to keep all the words of this law and these statutes, to do them: That his heart be not lifted up above his brethren, and that he turn not aside from the commandment, to the right hand, or to the left: to the end that he may prolong his days in his kingdom, he, and his children, in the midst of Israel.

» Studying God's Word is the natural response of a sincere Christian:

- 2 Tim 2: 15 Study to shew thyself approved unto God, a workman that needeth not to be ashamed, rightly dividing the word of truth.

IT BRINGS SPIRITUAL GROWTH

» **It grows YOU as a Christian**. Saturating your life with God's Word will allow the Spirit to change you from the inside out in ways that you never thought possible and in ways you could never have changed by yourself. The Bible is the agent by which spiritual growth happens:

- 1 Peter 2:2-3. As newborn babes, desire the sincere milk of the word, that ye may grow thereby: If so be ye have tasted that the Lord is gracious.

- Psalm 1 Blessed is the man that walketh not in the counsel of the ungodly, nor standeth in the way of sinners, nor sitteth in the seat of the scornful. But his delight is in the law of the Lord; and in his law doth he meditate day and night. And he shall be like a tree planted by the rivers of water, that bringeth forth his fruit in his season; his leaf also shall not wither; and whatsoever he doeth shall prosper.

» **It grows IN you as you grow.** Not only does it change you, but it multiplies itself from something small to something great:

- Luke 8:11. Now the parable is this: The seed is the word of God.

» **It guides you with supernatural wisdom.** This not only affects our day-to-day lives, but the overall direction our lives.

- Psalm 32:8. I will instruct thee and teach thee in the way which thou shalt go: I will guide thee with mine eye.

- Psalm 119:99. I have more understanding than all my teachers: for thy testimonies are my meditation.

- Proverbs 1:6. To understand a proverb, and the interpretation; the words of the wise, and their dark sayings.

- Psalm 119:105. Thy word is a lamp unto my feet, and a light unto my path.

- John 10:27. My sheep hear my voice, and I know them, and they follow me:

IT MAKES SENSE

Reading your Bible is a rational choice. Want "your best life now?" It's only accomplished through one means: knowing God. It's logical. If you're calling yourself a Christian and DON'T want to read the Bible, something is wrong with your understand of these points:

» **It's God's Word.** If you believe in God... well... um... why wouldn't you want Him to talk to you? Our Bible is "God-breathed," as if God wrote a love letter just for you:

- 2 Timothy 3:16. All scripture is given by inspiration of God, and is profitable for doctrine, for reproof, for correction, for instruction in righteousness:

» **If you say you love Him...**

- John 14:23-24. Jesus answered and said unto him, If a man love me, he will keep my words: and my Father will love him, and we will come unto him, and make our abode with him. He that loveth me not keepeth not my sayings: and the word which ye hear is not mine, but the Father's which sent me.

» **It's eternal.** Something that will be around forever is pretty special. No... diamonds aren't forever (sorry!), but God's Word is!

- Matthew 24:35. Heaven and earth shall pass away, but my words shall not pass away.

- Psalm 119:89. For ever, O Lord, thy word is settled in heaven.

- Psalm 119:151-153. Thou art near, O Lord; and all thy commandments are truth. Concerning thy testimonies, I have known of old that thou hast founded them for ever. Consider mine affliction, and deliver me: for I do not forget thy law.

» **It tells us more about God.** If you want to know God, get to know Him through His Word. Sure, nature can tell us *about* God, but the Word of God is knowing God himself.

- Romans 10:17. So then faith cometh by hearing, and hearing by the word of God.

» It tells us more about Jesus. God is revealed through creation, through His Word, and through His Son. Paul desired to see "Christ in you," when he wrote to the Colossian believers. The Bible helps us know Jesus:

- John 14:6. Jesus saith unto him, I am the way, the truth, and the life: no man cometh unto the Father, but by me.

- John 5:38-41. And ye have not his word abiding in you: for whom he hath sent, him ye believe not. Search the scriptures; for in them ye think ye have eternal life: and they are they which testify of me. And ye will not come to me, that ye might have life. I receive not honour from men.

- John 1:1-4. In the beginning was the Word, and the Word was with God, and the Word was God. The same was in the beginning with God. All things were made by him; and without him was not any thing made that was made. In him was life; and the life was the light of men.

- 1 Corinthians 15:1-4. Moreover, brethren, I declare unto you the gospel which I preached unto you, which also ye have received, and wherein ye stand; By which also ye are saved, if ye keep in memory what I preached unto you, unless ye have believed in vain. For I delivered unto you first of all that which I also received, how that Christ died for our sins according to the scriptures; And that he was buried, and that he rose again the third day according to the scriptures:

» **God's Word is truth.** Anyone seeking truth should dive into the book that claims to be the source of truth itself. We have no right to demand "truthfulness" from people without first being connected to the objective source of truth: God's Word.

- John 17:17. Sanctify them through thy truth: thy word is truth.

» **It shows God's will.** You don't have to search too much for God's will. You're in God's will when you obey God's Word:

- Psalm 40:7-8. Then said I, Lo, I come: in the volume of the book it is written of me, I delight to do thy will, O my God: yea, thy law is within my heart.

» **It's spending time with God.** I mean, come on, right? Hanging out with the Creator? He who knows me best yet loves me most? Amazing.

- Proverbs 2:6-7. For the Lord giveth wisdom: out

of his mouth cometh knowledge and understanding. He layeth up sound wisdom for the righteous: he is a buckler to them that walk uprightly.

IT'S A GOOD IDEA

IT'S SPIRITUALLY ENRICHING. Not only does God grow us and change us as we read and study the Word, He makes everything better in the process.

» **It's encouraging.** Want to be encouraged? Read the Bible. It gives hope and life:

- Romans 15:4. For whatsoever things were written aforetime were written for our learning, that we through patience and comfort of the scriptures might have hope.

- Psalm 119:50. This is my comfort in my affliction: for thy word hath quickened me.

» **It's the source of the fullest life**. God's Word enriches your life from top to bottom, inside out.

- Matthew 4:4. But he answered and said, It is written, Man shall not live by bread alone, but by every word that proceedeth out of the mouth of God.

- Matthew 7:24-25. Therefore whosoever heareth these sayings of mine, and doeth them, I will liken him unto a wise man, which built his house upon a rock: And the rain descended, and the floods came, and the winds blew, and beat upon that house; and it fell not: for it was founded upon a rock.

- Joshua 1:8. This book of the law shall not depart out of thy mouth; but thou shalt meditate therein day and night, that thou mayest observe to do according to all that is written therein: for then thou shalt make thy way prosperous, and then thou shalt have good success.

- John 6:63. It is the spirit that quickeneth; the flesh profiteth nothing: the words that I speak unto you, they are spirit, and they are life.

» **It makes you free.** Many people feel trapped in life. God's Word makes us free:

- John 8:31-32. Then said Jesus to those Jews which believed on him, If ye continue in my word, then are ye my disciples indeed; And ye shall know the truth, and the truth shall make you free.

» **It helps you stay in love with God**. Getting bored with Christianity? Then read the Word!

- Psalm 103:20-21. Bless the Lord, ye his angels, that excel in strength, that do his commandments, hearkening unto the voice of his word. Bless ye the Lord, all ye his hosts; ye ministers of his, that do his pleasure.

- Psalm 56:10-11. In God will I praise his word: in the Lord will I praise his word. In God have I put my trust: I will not be afraid what man can do unto me.

- Psalm 106:1-2. Praise ye the Lord. O give thanks unto the Lord; for he is good: for his mercy endureth for ever. Who can utter the mighty acts of the Lord? who can shew forth all his praise?

IT HELPS OUR EVERYDAY LIVES. Some of the Bible is just plain common sense. It hits us here we live—in our day-to-day choices. The hidden man of the heart is crucial, but it always flows out into life. The Bible affects not only the unseen changes, but the everyday ones, too.

» **It is good discipline.** Anything worth doing will take work. Reading the Bible is simple, but it isn't easy. Even in the daily discipline, though, there's value. Things that feel bad can many times be good:

- Hebrews 12:11. Now no chastening for the present seemeth to be joyous, but grievous: nevertheless afterward it yieldeth the peaceable fruit of righteousness unto them which are exercised thereby.

- 1 Corinthians 9:27. But I keep under my body, and bring it into subjection: lest that by any means, when I have preached to others, I myself should be a castaway.

» **Ignoring it is dumb.** I don't have a reference on this one. It's just a fine statement.

» **It helps you see Satan's traps.** Spiritual eyes are required to see the potholes in the road. The Bible gives us God's vision for our lives:

- Eph. 6:10-18. Finally, my brethren, be strong in the Lord, and in the power of his might. Put on the whole armour of God, that ye may be able to stand against the wiles of the devil. For we wrestle not against flesh and blood, but against principalities, against powers, against the rulers of the darkness of this world, against spiritual wickedness in high places. Wherefore take unto you the whole armour of God, that ye may be able to withstand in the evil day, and having done all, to stand. Stand therefore, having your loins girt about with truth, and having on the breastplate of righteousness; And your feet shod with the preparation of the gospel of peace; Above all, taking the shield of faith, wherewith ye shall be able to quench all the fiery darts of the wicked. And take the helmet of salvation, and the sword of the Spirit, which is the word of God: Praying always with all prayer and supplication in the Spirit, and watching thereunto with all perseverance and supplication for all saints;

» **It keeps us from "settling" for second-best.** Daily Bible reading refocuses your mind on the most important things—those critical to eternity.

- God warned about letting life "settle" too much: Zephaniah 1:12. And it shall come to pass at that time, *that* I will search Jerusalem with candles, and punish the men that are settled on their lees: that say in their heart, The LORD will not do good, neither will he do evil.

- Revelation 2:4. Nevertheless I have somewhat against thee, because thou hast left thy first love.

- Romans 12:11. Not slothful in business; fervent in spirit; serving the Lord;

- Proverbs 28:9. He that turneth away his ear from hearing the law, even his prayer shall be abomination.

» **It helps you spot false teaching.** We should read and study the Bible because there is so much false teaching.

- 1 Thessalonians 5:20–22. Despise not prophesyings. Prove all things; hold fast that which is good. Abstain from all appearance of evil.

» **It confronts us of sin.** God's Word confronts our sin and helps us get rid of it:

- Psalm 119:9-12. Wherewithal shall a young man cleanse his way? by taking heed thereto according to thy word. With my whole heart have I sought thee: O let me not wander from thy commandments. Thy word have I hid in mine heart, that I might not sin against thee. Blessed art thou, O Lord: teach me thy statutes.

» **It's more powerful than anything you'll ever do** (college education, job, money...)

- Hebrews 4:12. For the word of God is quick, and powerful, and sharper than any twoedged sword, piercing even to the dividing asunder of soul and spirit, and of the joints and marrow, and is a discerner of the thoughts and intents of the heart.

» **It's more valuable than anything you'll ever own** (phone, house, company...)

- Psalm 19:10-11. More to be desired are they than gold, yea, than much fine gold: sweeter also than honey and the honeycomb. Moreover by them is thy servant warned: and in keeping of them there is great reward.

There are 168 hours in a week. A SLOW reader can get through the Bible in a year and still have plenty of time for everything else in life. Commit to reading every day!

Here are a few closing thoughts from my dad, Pastor W. M. Rench:

» The Bible is alive and will talk with you.

» Your comprehension changes with life experience.

» Meanings change over time. In health, a text will mean something different to you in sickness, for example.

» The Bible becomes more comprehendible over the years of rereading it.

» The Bible takes on more significance if you hear it taught or preached later.

» The Bible is for ALL of us.

» The Bible is effectual when mixed with faith in the reader.

» Read even when you don't understand what you're reading.

» Read looking for God to speak to you personally.

» Read looking for Biblical principles.

» Read with intent to respond.

About the Author

Author's Words: I repeatedly demand that my teens call me *The Pope of Temecula*. They smirk and pat my bald spot with a condescending "There, there, Brother Ryan…" I'm the bigger man. I don't get mad. I'll accept *youth pastor* as my title instead.

Stuffy Bio: Ryan Rench serves as the youth director and associate pastor of Calvary Baptist Church in Temecula, CA, under his father's leadership, Pastor W. M. Rench. Ryan's family moved to Temecula in 1986 to plant the church where Ryan was reared and is now on staff. He earned his Bachelor's and Master's Degree in ministry from Heartland Baptist Bible College and Graduate School in 2008 and 2010.

Ryan Rench married his wife, Jamie, in 2008. They have one son named Abe (July 2012) and two daughters: Charlotte (March 2014) and Gwen (February 2016).

Ryan blogs at RyanRench.com and has published several books, including *BIBS: Big Idea Bible Study* and *A Case For Bible College*, available from **Calvary Baptist Publications** (CalvaryBaptist.pub.)

Let's Connect!

One cool thing about no-name authors (me) is that they are readily accessible. If you contact me, I'll respond. In fact, I'll probably be giddy. Usually it's only my wife and mom who read my stuff, and even THAT is hit and miss (I force them to proof my books just so I know they've read them). **Here's where I live:**
- **Email**: RyanRench@gmail.com (this is the TOP contact)
- **The Twitters**: @RyanARench (the Twitters is my fav!)
- **FaceBooks**: /RyanRenchcom (I sort of know how to work the FaceBooks. Sort of.)
- **Website**: RyanRench.com (my other contact info is here)

More Books
from CalvaryBaptist.pub

THE CHRISTIAN TEEN DEVOTIONAL
This is a collection of almost 200 notes from 7 years as a youth pastor.

"A CASE FOR" MINIBOOK SERIES
Dating God's Way. Several tips on following God's leading in dating.
Sunday Evening Church. Why our church loves our evening services.
Reverence. Why reverence is not a bad thing—when done right.
Saturday Soul-Winning. Some benefits of regular Saturday outreach.
Why We Have Church. A doctrinal and practical look at the institution of the church.

A CASE FOR BIBLE COLLEGE
Are you considering Bible college? This book covers:
1) *Why* we encourage high school graduates to attend a year of Bible college, and
2) *How to prepare* for Bible college once you have committed.

THE ILLUSTRIOUS #BIBSWALL

HOW TO BUILD THIS WALL

Each day you complete, you are awarded a brick in the wall. Color it to your heart's content.

Get creative! Use different colors, doodle some cool patterns, or write in a reference each day. Go crazy!

Build it. Keep building from the ground up, and watch your wall fill in day by day.

Upgrades. Watch for worker upgrades as you progress. You might get some extra help along the way!

#BIBSWALL

How's your wall coming along? Post a picture of it on social media and see what others have done.

A Daily and Weekly Devotional

Made in the USA
San Bernardino, CA
13 February 2018